REPTILES & AMPHIBIANS

leaf frog

NATIONAL GEOGRAPHIC NATURE LIBRARY

REPTILES & AMPHIBIANS

NATIONAL GEOGRAPHIC NATURE LIBRARY

by Catherine Herbert Howell

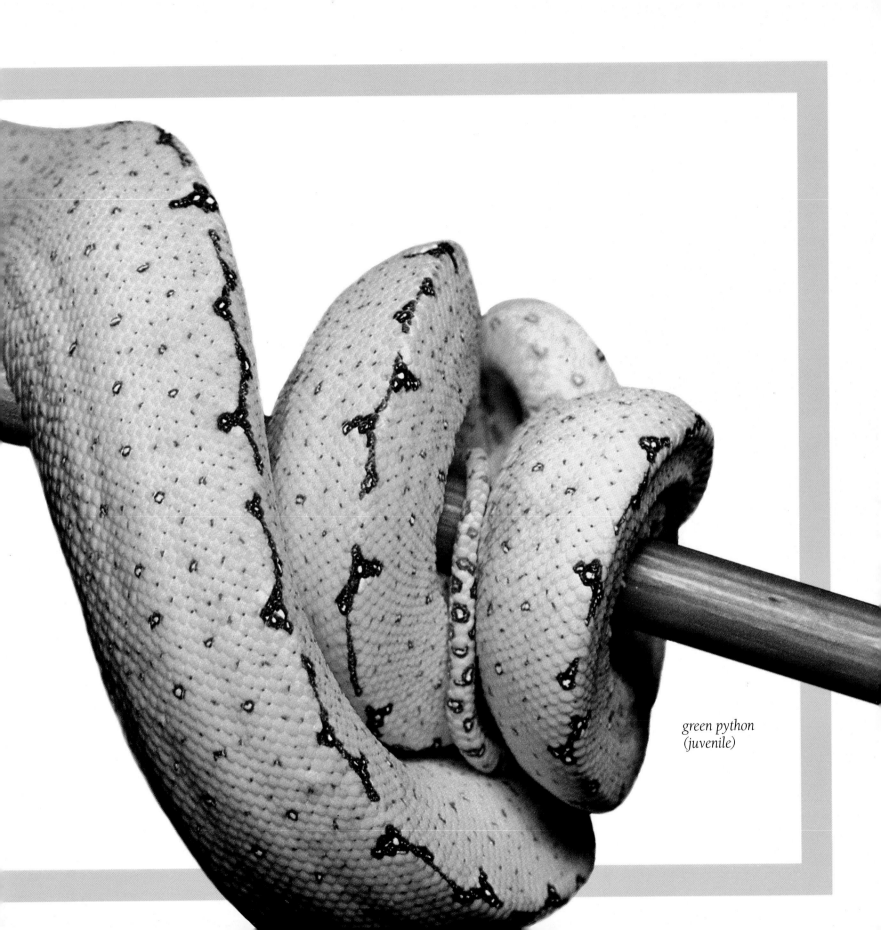

*green python
(juvenile)*

Table of Contents

marine iguana

anoles

green python

loggerhead turtle

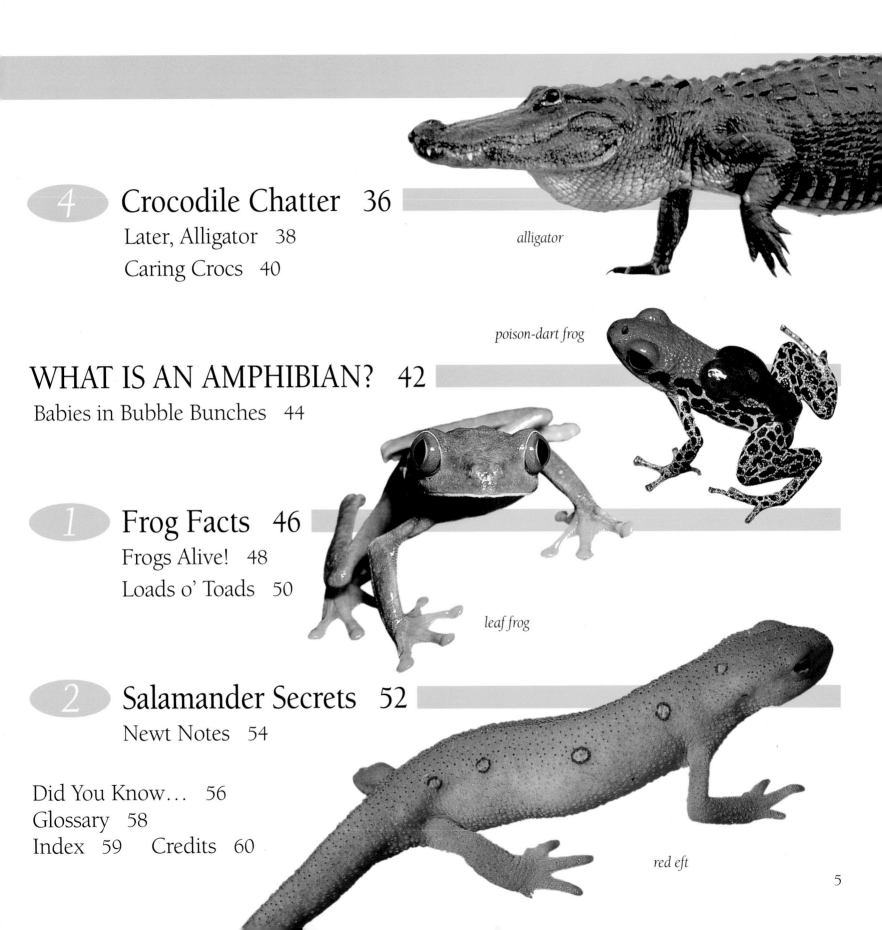

alligator

poison-dart frog

leaf frog

red eft

WHAT IS A REPTILE?

Reptiles have a bad reputation with some people, but they really are cool. There are four main groups of reptiles: lizards, snakes, turtles, and crocodilians. Another type, the tuatara (too-uh-TAR-uh), is the last of a large group of beak-headed reptiles that lived before the dinosaurs.

Reptiles may look very different from each other, but they are alike in these ways:

- They are VERTEBRATES (VURT-uh-bruts).
- They BREATHE AIR.
- They are COLD-BLOODED.
- They have DRY, SCALY SKIN.
- They hatch mostly from shelled EGGS LAID ON LAND.
- At birth, most LOOK LIKE THEIR PARENTS.

alligator

basilisk

water snake

tuatara

box turtle

Reptile Rap

What do a human and a reptile have in common? Each is a vertebrate—an animal with a backbone. Each breathes air, too, but these are the only obvious ways that you and a reptile are alike. Unlike you and other mammals, reptiles are cold-blooded. Their blood is not really cold, though. Cold-blooded animals control their body temperature by using sun and shade, rather than by sweating or panting as mammals do.

TOUGH EGGS
Most reptiles, like this coral snake, hatch from eggs that are leathery or hard or rubbery.

cooling off in the shade

HOT AND COOL DUDES
Reptiles need the sun's warmth to get moving. If the air is too hot, they beat it to a cooler spot.

ALL TUCKED IN ▶
Dry, shiny scales mark the skin of a tightly coiled pit viper. A reptile's skin holds in moisture and helps the animal survive in dry places.

HEADS UP!
River turtles and caimans (KAY-muns) both need to come up for air from time to time.

warming up in the sun

A backbone allows vertebrates to bend and twist.

1 Lizard Lingo

Lizards live all over the world—on every continent except Antarctica. They are at home in the trees or on the ground. One species, or kind, even swims in the sea. Lizards may be as small as your thumb or as long as a diving board. They may look like worms or like aliens from outer space. All 3,000 or so species of lizards have dry, scaly skin and some kind of tail.

Anoles inhabit the West Indies, Central and South America, and the southern United States.

A male anole (uh-NO-lee) spreads its brightly colored throat fan to threaten rivals or impress females.

BY THE SEA
Marine iguanas, from the Galápagos Islands, swim with flat, paddle-like tails.

Expert climbers, geckos can walk upside down.

A chameleon (kuh-MEEL-yun) can change color and pattern in less than a minute.

By changing color, it may send warnings or love calls to other chameleons.

TINY CHAMELEON
One of the smallest lizards, a Brookesia is one of the many species of chameleons that live on the African island of Madagascar.

ALL KINDS OF LIZARDS
Lizards may be fat or skinny, plain or colorful. They may have long legs or short ones—or none at all.

AWESOME DRAGON
World's largest kind of lizard, a ten-foot-long Komodo (KUH-moh-doh) dragon patrols the beach of its island home in Southeast Asia.

11

Fancy Footwork

Like kids, many lizards are good at running and climbing, but some lizards can do incredible things that a kid cannot. They can glide through the air, scamper up a wall, and scoot upside down along the ceiling. Because it has broad soles and fringed toe scales, a basilisk can skim across water for short distances! Special lizard feet make special lizard feats possible.

WIGGLE WALK
Like most lizards, an alligator lizard travels on all four feet and walks with a wiggle. This lizard, which lives in Venezuela, uses its long tail as a fifth leg to help it climb.

HANG IN THERE
Claw-like toes help a Jackson's chameleon hang on tightly.

Chameleon eyes, protected by a layer of skin, can spot even the slightest movement nearby.

On each foot, two pairs of toes facing in opposite directions give a chameleon a V-shaped grip.

QUICK GETAWAY ▶
The South American basilisk sprints on its hind legs. Reaching water, it runs right over the surface. When it slows down, it will fall in and start swimming.

12

IT'S A BIRD! IT'S A PLANE!

It's *Draco,* the flying dragon from Southeast Asia. Spreading its "wings," this lizard can glide more than 50 feet.

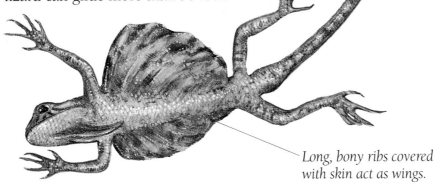

Long, bony ribs covered with skin act as wings.

IGUANA   GECKO

NEAT FEET

Using its sharp nails and long, spreading toes, an iguana clings to a leaf. Tiny split hairs on its overlapping toe pads help a gecko stick like Velcro to ceilings and walls.

Tongues Flicking, Tails Wagging

With their tongues and tails, lizards can do amazing things. Some species catch bugs with a zap of their long, sticky tongues. Others use their tongues to scare off enemies. Many lizards can ditch their tails when the going gets tough and grow them back later. Some can hold their tails straight out for balance or even wrap them around branches as monkeys do.

Look-alike head and tail keep enemies guessing.

The Australian shingleback's stumpy tail may store fat to be used as food during the winter.

ZAP IT!

A Parson's chameleon, from Madagascar, shoots out its tongue to catch a grasshopper. A sticky bulb on the end traps the prey, and the tongue reels it in.

BLUE-TONGUED SKINK

The Western skink, from North America, loses its bright tail color as it grows older.

BLUE BLUFF

A young Western skink can drop a piece of its blue tail and run while the still-wriggling piece distracts an enemy. An Australian blue-tongued skink wags its tongue and hisses at predators.

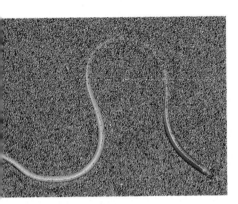

LONG AND LEAN
It may look like a worm or a tail left behind, but it's really a legless lizard from Africa's Namib Desert. Smooth, hard scales allow this kind of skink to slither easily through the sand.

A chameleon's tongue can reach farther than its body length.

crack

DITCH IT!
Weak points in the backbone mark places where a lizard's tail can neatly pull apart. The tail grows back, but it never looks the same.

BREAK DANCER
Strutting its stuff, a chameleon uses its tail as a helping hand when balancing on a thin branch.

15

The Better To See You

Most lizards see very well, some in daylight and some at night. They can use their eyes to track things that are far away. For slow-moving lizards, such as chameleons, good vision means the difference between life and death. Most lizards see in color, and some can change their body color to send each other messages.

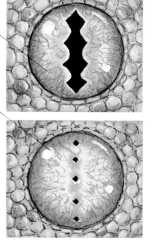

nighttime

daytime

Changes in the cells of its scales make a male agama (uh-GAHM-uh) blush when attracting a mate or fighting rivals.

MIRROR, MIRROR
A pardalis chameleon, another species from Madagascar, colors up to face the "foe" in the mirror.

EYE TO EYE
At night, a gecko's pupils open wide to let in more light. By day, they close down to a row of tiny holes.

huge eyes for hunting insects at night

THERE YOU ARE! ▶
A chameleon can see things coming and going. Its eyes swivel separately, and it can look in two directions at once.

BUG EYES
Unlike most lizards, a gecko has no eyelids. It uses its long tongue to keep its eyes free of dirt. Geckos live in the tropics all over the world.

16

Watch Out!

Lizards have to defend themselves from hungry predators and nasty neighbors. Speedy lizards can often run away. Slower ones change color, keep still, or dig a hole. For some species, a scary appearance—spikes, spines, horns, and crests—may make them look big and mean enough to fool their enemies.

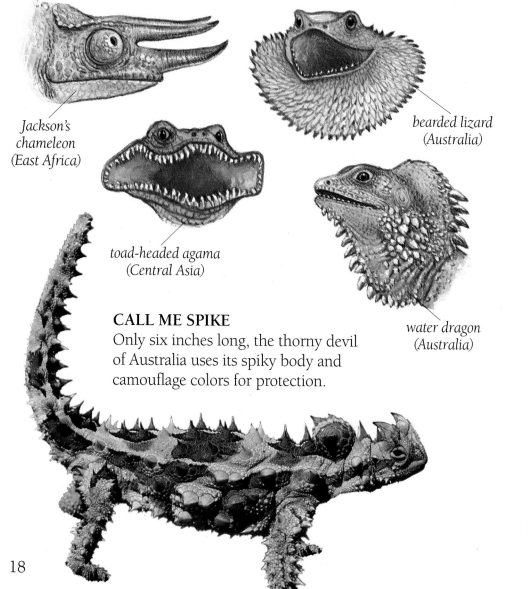

Jackson's chameleon (East Africa)

toad-headed agama (Central Asia)

bearded lizard (Australia)

water dragon (Australia)

CALL ME SPIKE
Only six inches long, the thorny devil of Australia uses its spiky body and camouflage colors for protection.

BUG OFF! ▶
When alarmed, the Australian frilled lizard makes itself look larger by spreading its frill, a ruffled collar of skin, and opening its mouth wide. Usually, the frill lies folded around the neck and shoulders.

AMAZONIAN ANOLE

COLOR ME SAFE
An anole blends with leaves on the rain forest floor. A leaf-tailed gecko matches the lichen (LY-kun) and bark on the trees it climbs.

LEAF-TAILED GECKO (AUSTRALIA)

2 Snake Scoop

Cold and slimy is how some people think of snakes. They are cold-blooded, but they are covered with smooth, dry scales—not slime. Scales contain the same protein found in your fingernails. Some snakes have a poisonous bite. Most do not, but they have other ways to get their food.

TWISTER
Hundreds of vertebrae, small bones in its back, make a snake the most flexible animal with a backbone.

All pit vipers have a heat-sensitive pit between each eye and nostril that helps them locate and zero in on warm-blooded prey.

GANG'S ALL HERE!
Garter snakes, found in North and Central America, gather in groups during mating season in the spring. Sometimes thousands huddle together underground in winter when hibernating. But most of the time, snakes are loners.

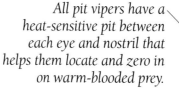

A West Indian thread snake may be only five inches long and as wide as the lead of a thick pencil.

Its green color camouflages
the tree-dwelling palm viper
in the rain forest of Costa Rica.

MEAN AND GREEN
A palm viper rests motionless
in a tree. If a bird comes near,
the snake will strike. Vipers
inject strong poison with a bite.

SNEAK IN SAND
Burrowing in the
desert sand of North
Africa, a horned viper
hides from its prey.
Lizards, watch out!

A giant anaconda, one of
the world's largest snakes,
may grow to more than
30 feet. It lives in swampy
areas of northern and
central South America.

Chowing Down

Snakes lack legs and arms, but they have ways to get meat to eat. Snakes called constrictors coil around prey and squeeze until breathing stops. Other species kill with a poisonous bite. Some will attack almost any animal of the right size, but many prefer a particular kind of prey.

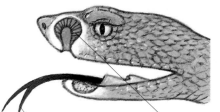

Forked tongue collects chemical signals from the air and from objects.

Jacobson's organ identifies the signals.

SNAKE SENSE
Tastes and smells alert a snake to food, danger, or company. Information gathered by its tongue and "read" by its Jacobson's organ helps a snake sense the world around it.

SO LONG, SNAIL
This South American snail-eating snake will stick out its lower jaw to scoop the animal out of its shell.

THE BIG SQUEEZE
A rat snake coils around a rat to suffocate and eat it.

OPEN WIDE!
A rat snake stretches its jaws around a soft-shelled egg. Like most snakes, it has a varied diet. The African egg-eating snake is pickier. Its body has adaptations that allow it to eat its main food—bird eggs.

The egg-eating snake has tooth-like spines for cracking hard shells.

Its neck muscles crush and squeeze out the shell as the snake swallows the egg.

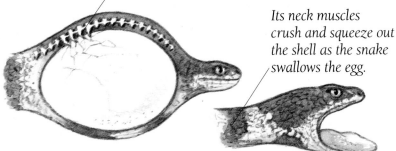

UP FRONT

A front-fanged snake delivers deadly venom, or poison, from sacs on each side of its head. A snake with especially long front fangs keeps them folded up until it is ready to strike.

front fangs

rear fang

sac for storing venom

BACK BITER

With its mouth open wide, a green parrot snake from Costa Rica puts on a threat display. This snake has rear fangs, which it uses to chew mild venom into its prey.

Grooving Along

Without legs to travel on, how do snakes get from here to there? Most have wide scales called scutes on their undersides. These overlap like shingles on a roof. Their back edges catch and hold the ground as muscles pull the snake forward.

Pythons and other thick-bodied snakes creep along almost in a straight line. Their belly scutes work like the treads of a tank. Some push back while others slide forward.

When disturbed, a cobra raises its upper body and spreads special ribs to form a scary hood.

SCALY "SCUTER"
Overlapping belly scutes are attached by muscles to this Indian cobra's many pairs of ribs.

FLYING HIGH
The flying snake flattens its body to glide from branch to branch. It lives in Southeast Asia.

A cobra can continue to move forward when raised to strike.

SNAKY SWIMMER
Its flat, paddle-like tail propels a sea snake through the warm water it inhabits.

SLINKY SNAKE
To climb a tree, a rat snake moves like an accordion, scrunching its body and gripping with its tail. The snake's head stretches forward, and the rest of its body catches up.

24

SIDEWINDER

To keep from slipping on loose sand, a sidewinding adder swings its head and upper body forward and sideways. Its lower body and tail follow, with its belly raised above the hot sand. This Namibian snake sidewinds again and again, leaving J-shaped tracks.

ROCKY ROAD

A garter snake pushes against stones, plants, or anything else in its path, making an "S" with its body as it moves along.

25

Hide and Seek

Soldiers dress in camouflage to hide from their enemies. Many snakes use camouflage, too. Their colors blend with their surroundings. If the snakes keep very still, they seem part of the scenery. Some harmless species have the same colors as certain poisonous snakes and may fool enemies into thinking they are poisonous, too.

PYTHON   PUFF ADDER

SCALE TALE
Snake scales may be small, smooth, and shiny, like those of a South African python, or larger, with ridges, like the ones of the West African puff adder.

Learn and beware:
Red touch yellow
—kill a fellow.
Red touch black
—friend of Jack.

milk snake

coral snake

COPYCAT
In the southern United States, a harmless milk snake wears the same color rings as the poisonous Eastern coral snake. But look closely— the pattern of their rings is different.

SAND TRAP
A desert viper of Namibia matches the sand where it hides. Eyes on top of its head watch for prey.

WHAT SNAKE?
Its colors and pattern make a Gaboon viper seem to disappear among the dead leaves of its African rain forest home.

YELLOW FELLOW
Looped around golden palm fruit, a poisonous eyelash viper of Costa Rica waits for prey to come near.

ON THE LOOKOUT
Snakes never close their eyes, even when they sleep, because they do not have eyelids. Instead of a lid, each eye has a clear scale that protects it.

Ready, Set, Grow!

Most snakes hatch from tough, leathery eggs laid on land. The eggshells stretch and bend as the embryos, or young, grow inside. The shells may swell up to twice the size they were when laid. A few snakes develop in their mother's body and are born live. All newborn snakes are ready to survive on their own. As a snake grows, its skin stretches but cannot grow. So from time to time, the snake sheds its tight suit. Underneath is a shiny new one.

Fluid that cushioned the embryo bubbles out of a hole the baby snake makes.

A snake uses its egg tooth to slit open its shell.

flexible shell

EGG OR NOT?
Through an opening in its mother's belly, a Costa Rican hog-nosed viper is born. A North American black racer guards her eggs until they hatch.

HELLO, WORLD!
A baby green mamba of Africa pokes out of its egg. Like other snakes, it has one tiny egg tooth at the front of its mouth. This tooth will drop off in about a week. The baby snake keeps its other teeth, growing new ones if any are lost.

SNAKE A-PEEL

Snake skin becomes dull looking just before it is shed. The thick outer skin has two layers. Shedding occurs when the top layer separates from the one underneath it.

A snake does not lose its color as it sheds because most of its color cells lie in a deeper layer of skin.

Shed skin still shows scales and details.

A South African tiger snake wears its new skin.

RATTLE TAIL

When a rattlesnake shakes its tail, the rattle on the end clicks and buzzes.

When this North American snake sheds, it adds a new section to its rattle.

HEAD FIRST

Starting at the head, a North American corn snake begins to shed. Even the old eye scales peel off.

29

Turtle Talk

Turtles live in almost any kind of habitat—fields, forests, deserts, swamps, ponds, rivers, and the sea. Tortoises are land turtles, and terrapins are freshwater turtles. Turtles can live longer than any other vertebrates, including humans.

TIGHT FIT ▶
A box turtle can close up its shell tighter than any other turtle. It loves to eat grasses, fruits, insects, and worms, and may eat so much that it grows almost too fat for its shell.

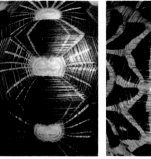
RADIATED TORTOISE   STAR TORTOISE

SHELL ART
The shells of radiated and star tortoises display beautiful patterns.

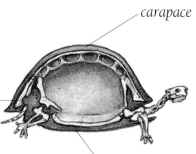

carapace

backbone

plastron

MOBILE HOME
Its shell is part of its skeleton, so a turtle can never leave it. The only reptile with a shell, a turtle carries its home with it wherever it goes.

UP PERISCOPE
To look around, a North American box turtle stretches out its neck. If alarmed, it will scrunch its neck and pull its head into its shell.

SIDE TUCK
For protection, some tropical turtles bend their necks and heads to the side.

The helmeted turtle lives south of the Sahara in Africa.

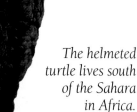

By Land and by Sea

A turtle's body is made for the way it lives. Land turtles have hard, rounded shells that they can hide in. Short, sturdy legs carry the shell's weight. Sea turtles have flatter, lighter shells and longer legs with webbed feet or flippers. They stay mostly in warm seas around the world.

A sea turtle snaps up fish with its beak.

Using its forked tail as a rudder, a frigatebird swoops down to snatch a baby turtle.

No matter where they live, all turtles lay their eggs on land. A female sea turtle will often return to the beach where she hatched to lay her own eggs.

RISKY BUSINESS

Newly hatched sea turtles race to the water to avoid birds and other enemies. A nest may have up to 200 hatchlings, but they face many dangers. Only a few will make the short trip safely.

At night, when the hatchlings begin their trip to the sea, they look for a bright horizon. Sometimes they get confused and head toward the lights of houses—away from the sea, the only place where they can survive.

Its streamlined shell allows this loggerhead turtle to slip easily through the water.

rear flippers used mainly for steering

UNDER THE SEA

Sea turtles spend most of their lives in water. They cannot pull completely into their flat shells to protect their head and limbs, but strong flippers help them swim fast to escape danger.

GENTLE GIANT

A Galápagos tortoise has strong, scaly legs to hold up its heavy, domed body. An old male may grow almost four feet long and weigh 500 to 600 pounds—more than twice as much as a female.

Capable of living more than 150 years, these tortoises are now endangered on their island home off South America.

front flippers used for swimming

33

Odd Turtle Out

Some of the first turtles were neighbors of the dinosaurs. Many species still look like creatures of long ago. Some are common, like the familiar box turtle that may visit your yard. Others live in only a few places around the world.
Turtles come in many sizes and shapes, and some have strange features or habits that help them survive in their environment.

Soft-shelled turtles can be found in Africa, Asia, Indonesia, and North America. Their flat shells help them hide in the sand and mud of river bottoms.

RUBBERNECKER
The Australian snake-necked turtle can stick its long neck into rocky crevices to catch its dinner. It feeds on fish, snails, and shrimps.

Check out the wiggly pink tip of the alligator snapping turtle's tongue! The fish will find out—too late—that it is not a worm.

KISSING COUSINS
World's largest tortoise, the Aldabra may weigh 560 pounds. It roams an island in the Indian Ocean. A speckled Cape tortoise of South Africa weighs less than one pound.

TURTLE PARADE

Special adaptations help turtles find food or avoid danger. The big-headed turtle cannot pull its oversize head into its shell for safety, but its head is covered with armor.

A stinkpot drives away enemies by giving off a yucky smell. Fringes of skin on the long neck of a matamata feel the water ripple when a fish swims near. The turtle then opens its huge mouth and sucks in the prey.

big-headed turtle
(Southeast Asia)

matamata
(South America)

stinkpot
(eastern United States)

TURTLE TRICKERY

The alligator snapping turtle inhabits slow-moving rivers in the southeastern United States. Sitting very still with its mouth open, the turtle waits for prey on river bottoms. Tiny plants called algae (AL-jee) often grow on its shell and camouflage it.

35

4 Crocodile Chatter

Alligators, crocodiles, and gharials (GAR-ee-ulls) make up the crocodilians. These reptiles live in warm areas of the world, never far from water. Well suited for their wet and wild life-style, they have looked much the same for 65 million years. The largest crocodilians, saltwater crocodiles, range from western India to northern Australia.

GREEN SUBMARINE ▶
Eyes, ears, and nostrils on top of its snout allow this American alligator to see, hear, and breathe while floating in duckweed-covered water.

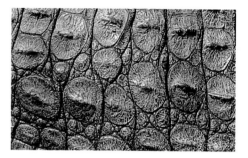

TOUGH SKIN
Crocodile scales do not overlap as a snake's do. A sharp, bony ridge strengthens some of the crocodile's back and tail scales.

Crocodilians paddle with their partly webbed feet when swimming slowly. Paddling also helps them keep their balance in the water.

The largest reptile, a saltwater crocodile may grow to 25 feet—as long as a small school bus.

POWER TAIL
Pushing with its powerful tail, an alligator speeds through the water. It moves like a snake, keeping its legs by its sides and aiming its head in the direction in which it is going.

Later, Alligator

Crocodilians have a lot in common. They are born small—some only ten inches long—but they grow fast. All have long bodies, flat heads, and cone-shaped teeth. To tell one from the other, check out their teeth and the shape of their snouts. Crocodilians grow new teeth in place of worn or lost ones. When they grow old, they can no longer replace their teeth. An old croc may have almost no teeth at all.

Plovers, also called "crocodile birds," act as feathered toothpicks for this African crocodile.

SAY "AAAH!"
Resting with its mouth open to cool off, a Nile crocodile attracts birds that pick meat, leeches, and insects from its teeth and skin.

CROCODILE
A crocodile's snout is narrower than an alligator's. When the jaws are closed, the fourth lower tooth on either side sticks up.

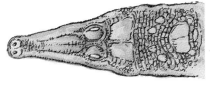

ALLIGATOR
An alligator's snout is usually wide and rounded. When the mouth is closed, all of the teeth point down.

GHARIAL
Found mostly in India, the gharial has a long, skinny snout. All of the gharial's teeth show when its mouth is shut.

THE BETTER TO BITE YOU
Strong jaws and sharp teeth give an American crocodile a powerful bite, but this ferocious-looking reptile cannot chew. It tears its prey and often swallows it whole.

A crocodile may grow up to 50 sets of new teeth in its lifetime.

stone stew for supper

Crocodilians often swallow stones and other hard objects, which may help their stomachs grind food.

Caring Crocs

Despite their fierce looks, female crocodilians, especially crocodiles, are caring mothers. Some lay their eggs in deep holes along shady riverbanks. Others build nests of rotting swamp plants. They all guard their nests against egg snatchers. After the babies hatch, they stick close to their mother for a few weeks or longer. Then the young may hide out for several years until they are big enough to defend themselves.

INSTANT SWIMMER
Unlike crocodile hatchlings, a baby alligator heads straight for the water all by itself after leaving its shell. It needs no lessons—it can already swim!

LET ME OUT!
A ten-inch-long crocodile climbs out of its three-inch-long egg. It has been curled up inside for about three months.

At hatching time, the baby croc grunts softly from inside its egg—a signal for its mother to uncover the nest. Like snakes, crocodilians are born with an egg tooth, which they use to slit open their shell.

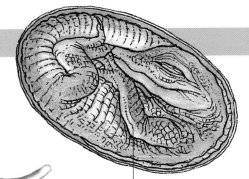

*baby croc
curled up
inside its shell*

TENDER TEETH
A Nile crocodile mother holds a hatchling carefully in her mouth while moving it to a nearby nursery marsh or pond. The mother has a throat pouch she can also use for carrying her young.

ALL ABOARD!
Mother is a jungle gym for crocodilian hatchlings. They swim with her, and she lets them crawl and rest on her head and back.

41

WHAT IS AN AMPHIBIAN?

There are three groups of amphibians: frogs and toads; salamanders and newts; and legless creatures called caecilians (si-SILL-yens). These creepy, crawly critters descended from fish. Amphibians were the first vertebrates—animals with backbones—to leave the water and live on land. Most amphibians metamorphose (met-uh-MOR-foze), or change form, as they grow.

Amphibians are alike in these ways:

- They are VERTEBRATES.
- They BREATHE AIR through their lungs and skin.
- They are COLD-BLOODED.
- They have SCALELESS SKIN.
- Most come from unshelled EGGS LAID IN MOIST PLACES.
- At birth, most DO NOT LOOK LIKE THEIR PARENTS.

caecilian

leopard frog

tadpoles

American toad

red salamander

salamander larvae

43

Babies in Bubble Bunches

The name "amphibian" means "double life." Most amphibians live part of their lives in water and part on land. They start out as eggs laid in or near fresh water. In their next stage, as larvae, they are water-dwellers that breathe through gills as fish do. They develop into adults that spend most of their time on land, taking in oxygen through their lungs and skin.

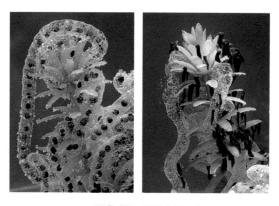

TOAD PEARLS
Long strings of toad eggs wind like necklaces around marsh plants. The embryos inside the eggs grow into tiny tadpoles.

JELLY BABIES
The pickerel frog of North America lays a clump of eggs in shallow water. The eggs do not have shells, but the embryos are protected by a clear jelly.

A rain froglet will emerge in several weeks, usually during a rain.

FROG MARBLES
Costa Rican rain froglets peer from their eggs, which were laid in moss growing on a tree or a log. Most frogs and toads grow into tadpoles, but rain frogs develop fully in their eggs. They change form before emerging.

PROTECTIVE PAPA ▶
The male glass frog of Central and South America guards eggs laid on a leaf by the female. Tadpoles develop and fall in the stream below.

METAMORPHOSIS

A frog goes through amazing
changes. An embryo
inside a jelly-coated egg
becomes a free-swimming,
fish-like tadpole with a tail.
Then, as legs develop,
the tail disappears. The frog
may take several years
to reach its full adult size.

45

Frog Facts

1

Many frogs are built for a double life—on land and in water. They breathe through their lungs and also through their smooth, moist skin. Frogs use their long, strong back legs to jump far and swim fast. Many can leap up to 20 times—a few even 40 times—their body length! The largest group of amphibians—about 3,850 species— frogs live on all continents except Antarctica.

Frogs come in all sizes and in all the colors of the rainbow.

LEAP, FROG!
Adult frogs, such as this tree frog, have no tail to get in the way when jumping. The frog can take off from a sitting position, then stretch its body out.

long back feet with flexible ankle joints

long, slender back legs ready to spring

DON'T TOUCH!
A poison-dart frog's brilliant color warns enemies that it is poisonous to eat.

Some South American Indians use fluid from the skin of these tree frogs to poison the tips of darts and arrows.

strong leg muscles

Short front legs help break the tree frog's fall when it lands.

Large, globe-shaped eyes give frogs a wide-angle view.

WIDE EYES

Like this red-eyed leaf frog of Central America, most frogs can see in all directions at the same time. Good vision helps them find food and spot enemies. Frogs can see in full color.

FAST FOOD

A green frog from eastern North America flicks its sticky tongue to catch a fly. In a flash, it will pull the fly in and swallow it whole. An insect is a frog's favorite food.

Sticky pads on the bottom of its toes allow a leaf frog to stick to a slippery stem.

Frogs Alive!

Tree frogs live in forests all over the world. They may be tiny—some less than an inch long—but they sure are talented. Long, skinny legs and sticky pads on their fingers and toes let them romp in the trees like acrobats. Most species of frogs sing, but usually only the males. Some have especially loud or musical voices. Others do not sing at all.

This European pond frog, also called an edible frog, has two vocal pouches, which balloon from the sides of its throat.

FROG FOAM
African gray tree frogs make a bubbly nest for their eggs on a branch. With their back legs, they whip up a thick white liquid that was released by the females.

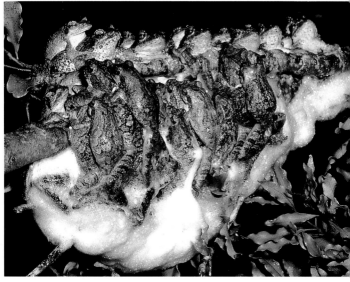

BOOM BOX
A male tree frog fills his vocal pouch with air to send a love call loud and clear.

single vocal pouch

HANGING OUT
The sun bakes the outside of the gray tree frogs' foam nest into a hard crust. Tadpoles grow inside, where it stays moist. When rain softens the nest, the tadpoles slowly sink to the bottom. Then they plop from the tree into the water below and swim away.

48

Two tadpoles ride piggyback on their parent. The adult is caring for them while they develop.

Tree frogs have grasping feet that help them cling to branches and leaves. On the ground, some tree frogs walk rather than hop as other frogs do.

BABY BACKPACK
A poison-dart frog may carry as many as 20 eggs on its back. It may be the mother or the father. When the tadpoles are grown and ready to swim, the parent will drop them off at a nearby pool of water.

The reticulated poison-dart frog lives in the rain forest of the Amazon River basin.

49

Loads o' Toads

Toads look a lot like their frog cousins, but they are different in some ways. With plumper bodies and shorter hind legs, toads are not as good jumpers as frogs. A toad's skin is dry, bumpy, and nasty to predators—but won't give you warts. Like frogs, most toads are active at night and stay close to home. They live just about everywhere frogs do.

YUMMM!
Hiding in a hollow log, a toad slurps up a worm. Farmers like toads because they also eat a lot of harmful insects.

Camouflaged by a leaf-like patch of yellow skin on its back, the Cameroon horned toad can hide from predators on the leafy forest floor of its African home.

BACHELOR PAD
Male golden toads gather at a pond, waiting for mates. Rarely seen, these tiny toads live only in the rain forest of Costa Rica. They may now be extinct.

TOUGH TOAD

A marine toad of Central America, also called a giant toad, puffs up to repel a snake. The poison in its skin is its best protection.

2

Salamander Secrets

Salamanders are quiet and shy, so scientists don't know as much about them as they do about other amphibians. Many salamanders come out only at night to hunt prey. Salamanders prefer to live where it is cool and damp. Many species live part of their life in water and part on land, and some spend their entire life on land. Still others never leave the water. Most species, such as the spotted salamander, spend much of their time under cover.

Salamanders usually have smooth, moist skin.

embryo inside the egg

gills for getting oxygen from the water

SUNNY SIDE UP

Most salamanders begin their lives in a clear, jelly-covered egg laid in water or in a damp place. Inside the egg, the embryo already has the basic body form of an adult. Warmed by the sun, it will wriggle free in a few weeks. The larva then swims away, with no parent to care for it.

WATER BABY

A newt larva finds food and shelter among water plants. It swims like a fish and breathes through feathery gills. Most salamanders live in water while changing for life on land. Their legs and lungs develop, and their gills slowly disappear.

The spotted salamander
is rarely seen
during its 20-year life
except at breeding time.

A salamander
keeps its tail
as an adult.

LANDLUBBER
Creature of the land, an adult
spotted salamander hides on the
damp floor of forests in eastern
North America. A good sense
of smell helps it find food and
a mate. In the spring, hundreds of
these salamanders come out
of hiding and return to their home
ponds to breed and lay eggs.

Salamanders can
grow a new part
of a damaged eye.

GOOGLY EYES
Eyes on top of its head help the
ensatina salamander of North America
spot prey in water. For protection,
it can pull its eyes into the sockets.

53

Newt Notes

Some salamanders, such as the red spotted newt, go through an additional stage in their life cycle. After it has been an egg, a swimming larva, and a land-living juvenile, or young, this newt returns to the water. To do all this, its body changes several times. Even its common name changes during metamorphosis.

Skin that is orangy-red, rough, dry—and poisonous— marks the red eft.

GHOSTLY NEWT

Shed skin drifts by a European crested newt. Newts, like other amphibians and reptiles, shed their skin as they grow. They usually eat the old skin.

PETER PAN ▶

Like that fairy-tale boy, the Mexican axolotl (ack-suh-LOT-uhl) never grows up. It looks and lives like a larva, but it can have young. Sometimes axolotls do complete the change into gill-less, land-dwelling adults.

FOUR-ACT PLAY

The red-spotted newt of eastern North America has a complicated life story. From egg to larva to red eft to newt, it moves from the water to the land, and, finally, back to the water to stay.

Act One: Tiny, jelly-covered egg develops underwater.

Act Two: Gilled larva emerges. Feeding on little insects, it grows and changes.

Act Three: Now a young red eft, it heads for the forest. There it will spend two or three years.

Act Four: An adult newt, slick and green, returns to the pond to breed.

Did You Know...

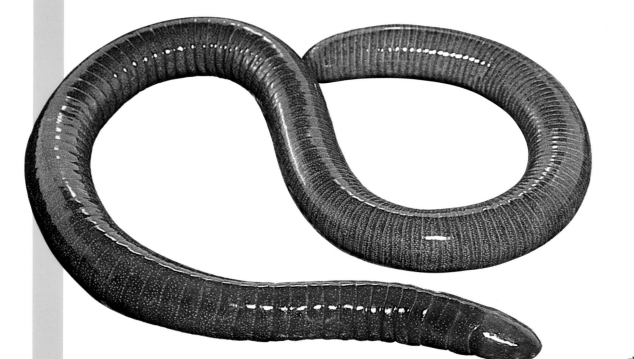

1 **THAT** what looks like a worm—but has a backbone and wriggles like a snake—is really a caecilian? Found in Asia, Africa, and Central and South America, these legless creatures are the only amphibians with scales. Some species live in the water, but most burrow underground, using their hard heads. Most are blind, but have an excellent sense of smell.

2 **THAT** the tuatara used to live all over the world, but today survives only on a few islands off New Zealand? The name of this lizard look-alike means "peaks on the back." Its closest relatives died out more than 135 million years ago.

3 **THAT** female sea turtles cry? It is not because they are sad, however. They weep big, salty tears when they crawl onto land to lay eggs. This helps their bodies get rid of extra salt from seawater.

4 **THAT** most tadpoles are the color of mud? But the tadpoles of this tree frog, which lives in a Costa Rican rain forest, are brightly colored.

5 **THAT** large snakes such as boas and pythons occasionally "pig out" on animals much larger than they are? An especially big meal can keep one of those snakes going for more than a year.

6 **THAT** some tree frogs in South America's Chaco desert region make their own moisture lotion? Their skin glands make a waxy substance that the frogs wipe all over their bodies to keep from drying out.

7 **THAT** the Gila (HEE-luh) monster of the southwestern United States and Mexico is one of only two kinds of poisonous lizards? The Gila monster poisons its victims slowly. First it bites them. Then it chews hard to make poison flow from its glands, through grooves in its teeth, into the prey.

Glossary

ADAPTATION A specialized body part—such as a tail or a tongue—or behavior that allows an animal to survive and reproduce in its environment.

ALGAE Simple forms of plant life, found mostly in water.

CAMOUFLAGE A natural disguise, such as skin color or pattern, that helps an animal blend with its surroundings.

COLD-BLOODED Having a body temperature that varies with the temperature of the surroundings.

CONSTRICTOR A type of snake that kills by suffocation, coiling its body tightly around its prey.

EMBRYO An animal in the early stages of development before birth or hatching.

EXTINCT No longer existing on the earth.

FANG A long, sharp tooth.

FLEXIBLE Elastic, able to bend.

GILLS The organs of fish and of amphibian larvae used for taking in oxygen from water.

HABITAT An animal's natural home, such as a river, a forest, or a desert.

HIBERNATE To enter an inactive, sleeplike state, with lowered body temperature, which aids survival in cold months.

JUVENILE A young, immature animal.

LARVA The first stage of an amphibian's life after it leaves the egg.

METAMORPHOSIS The rapid change in structure by an animal that has more than one body form during its life.

PREDATOR An animal that hunts and kills other animals for food.

PREY An animal that is hunted by other animals for food.

PROTEIN The main chemical material found in all living cells that contains carbon, hydrogen, nitrogen, and oxygen.

SCALE One of the small, flattened, hard plates that make up the thick outer skin of reptiles, fish, and birds' legs.

SPECIES A group of animals of the same kind that can produce young like themselves.

TADPOLE The larva of a frog or a toad.

VENOM A poisonous substance that is formed and transmitted by some animals, such as snakes and bees, usually by biting or stinging.

VERTEBRA One of the bony segments that make up the backbone, or spine.

VERTEBRATE An animal—fish, amphibian, reptile, bird, or mammal—with a backbone.

WARM-BLOODED Able to keep a constant body temperature even when the temperature of the surroundings varies.

Index

Boldface indicates illustrations.

COVER: Plumed basilisk, a member of the iguana family, lives in Central and South American rain forests.

Printed and bound by R.R. Donnelly & Sons Company, Willard, Ohio. Color separations by Graphic Art Service, Inc., Nashville, Tennessee, and Lincoln Graphics, Inc., Cherry Hill, New Jersey. Case cover printed by Inland Press, Menomonee Falls, Wisconsin.

Credits

horned frog

Published by
The National Geographic Society
Reg Murphy, *President*
    and Chief Executive Officer
Gilbert M. Grosvenor,
    Chairman of the Board
Nina D. Hoffman, *Senior Vice President*
William R. Gray, *Vice President and Director Book Division*
Barbara Lalicki, *Director of Children's Publishing*
Barbara Brownell, *Senior Editor*

Staff for this book
Toni Eugene, *Project Editor*
Jane H. Buxton, *Editor*
Marianne R. Koszorus, *Art Director*
John G. Agnone, *Illustrations Editor*
Elizabeth B. Booz, Alison J. Kahn, *Researchers*
Cinda Rose, Sharon Davis Thorpe, *Contributing Art Directors*
Heather Guwang, *Production Project Manager*
H. Robert Morrison, *Production*
Artemis S. Lampathakis, *Illustrations Assistant*
Karen F. Edwards, *Design Assistant*
Sandra F. Lotterman, Teresita Cóquia Sison, Marilyn J. Williams,
    Staff Assistants
Elisabeth MacRae-Bobynskyj, *Indexer*

Manufacturing and Quality Management
George V. White, *Director;* John T. Dunn, *Associate Director;*
    Vincent P. Ryan, *Manager;* and R. Gary Colbert

Acknowledgments

We are grateful for the assistance of Thomas A. Jenssen, Virginia Polytechnic Institute and State University; Ronald I. Crombie, W. Ronald Heyer, and George R. Zug, National Museum of Natural History, Smithsonian Institution, *Scientific Consultants.* We also thank Anna B. Blabey, Eleni Grove, and Edward Leber for their suggestions.

Illustrations Credits

Front Matter: COVER, 1, Michael & Patricia Fogden. 2-3, Gerry Ellis/THE WILDLIFE COLLECTION. 4 (top to bottom), Dieter & Mary Plage/SURVIVAL ANGLIA; Michael & Patricia Fogden; John Cancalosi/DRK PHOTO; Runk & Schoenberger/GRANT HEILMAN. 5 (top to bottom), John Cancalosi/TOM STACK & ASSOCIATES; Michael Fogden/DRK PHOTO; Michael & Patricia Fogden; George H. Harrison/GRANT HEILMAN. 6-7 (art), Tony Chen. 8 (art), Robert Cremins. 8 (left), Brian Rogers/BIOFOTOS. 8 (right), Michael & Patricia Fogden. 9 Seaphot Limited/PLANET EARTH PICTURES.

Lizards: 10-11 (art), Tony Chen. 10 Larry Minden/MINDEN PICTURES. 11 (left), José Azel/CONTACT PRESS IMAGES. 11 (right), Frans Lanting. 12 (left), Bruce Davidson/SURVIVAL ANGLIA. 12 (right), G.I. Bernard/OXFORD SCIENTIFIC FILMS. 12-13 Stephen Dalton/NHPA. 13 (art), Robert Cremins. 13 (center), ANIMALS ANIMALS/Stephen Dalton. 13 (right), Dwight R. Kuhn. 14-15 (art, all), Robert Cremins. 14-15, Frans Lanting/MINDEN PICTURES. 14 Stanley Breeden/DRK PHOTO. 15 (left), Michael & Patricia Fogden. 15 (right), Art Wolfe. 16 (art), Robert Cremins. 16 (left), Art Wolfe. 16 (right), Michael & Patricia Fogden. 17, J.B. Davidson. 18 (art), Robert Cremins. 18 (left), Densey Clyne/Mantis Wildlife Films/OSF. 18 (top, right), Jeff Foott/DRK PHOTO. 18 (bottom, right), Jean-Paul Ferrero/JACANA. 18-19, J. Cancalosi/DRK PHOTO.

Snakes: 20 and 21 (art), Robert Cremins. 20 François Gohier. 20-21, Michael Fogden/OXFORD SCIENTIFIC FILMS. 21 Philippe Varin/JACANA. 22 (art, top & bottom), Robert Cremins. 22 (art, center), Tony Chen. 22 (top left), Michael Fogden/OXFORD SCIENTIFIC FILMS. 22 (bottom left), ANIMALS ANIMALS/C.C. Lockwood. 23 (art), Robert Cremins. 23 Michael & Patricia Fogden. 24 & 25 (art), Robert Cremins. 24 Belinda Wright/DRK PHOTO. 25 Michael & Patricia Fogden. 26 (art, left), Robert Cremins. 26 (art, right), Tony Chen. 26 (left), ANIMALS ANIMALS/Anthony Bannister. 26 (top center), A. Kerneis-Dragesco/JACANA. 26 (top right), Anthony Bannister/NHPA. 27 (left), Michael & Patricia Fogden. 27 (right), Philip Sharpe/OXFORD SCIENTIFIC FILMS. 28 (left), Anthony Bannister/NHPA. 28 (top right), Michael Fogden/OXFORD SCIENTIFIC FILMS. 28 (center right), GRANT HEILMAN. 29 (art), Robert Cremins. 29 (center), Anthony Bannister/NHPA. 29 (right), ANIMALS ANIMALS/Zig Leszczynski.

Turtles: 30 (art), Robert Cremins. 30 (top left, both), Heather Angel. 30 (bottom left), Joe McDonald. 30 (bottom right), Anthony Bannister/NHPA. 30-31, Leonard Lee Rue/RUE ENTERPRISES. 32 (art), Tony Chen. 32, 32-33, Runk & Schoenberger /GRANT HEILMAN. 33 François Gohier. 34 (top art) and 35 (top art), Robert Cremins. 34 (left), Anthony Bannister/NHPA. 34 (right), Australasian Nature Transparencies/NHPA. 34-35 (art), Tony Chen.

Crocodilians: 36 (art), Robert Cremins. 36 (left), Stephen J. Krasemann/DRK PHOTO. 36 (right), G.I. Bernard/OXFORD SCIENTIFIC FILMS. 37, F. Stuart Westmorland/ALLSTOCK. 38-39 (art), Tony Chen.. 38-39, Stan Osolinski/OXFORD SCIENTIFIC FILMS. 39 (art center and bottom), Robert Cremins. 39 (right, top to bottom), Frans Lanting/MINDEN PICTURES; Art Wolfe; Art Wolfe. 40 (left), Fred Whitehead. 40-41, Frans Lanting/MINDEN PICTURES. 41 (art top), Robert Cremins. 41 (art bottom), Tony Chen. 41 Jonathan S. Blair.

Amphibians: 42-43 (art), Tony Chen. 44 (left), Rannels/GRANT HEILMAN. 44 (right both), Runk & Schoenberger/GRANT HEILMAN. 44 (bottom), Michael Fogden. 44-45 (left), Michael Fogden. 45 (art), Robert Cremins. 46-47 (art), Robert Cremins. 46-47, Stephen Dalton/NHPA. 46 (right), Art Wolfe. 47 (left), Runk & Schoenberger/GRANT HEILMAN. 47 (right), Michael & Patricia Fogden. 48 (art), Robert Cremins. 48 (all), Michael & Patricia Fogden. 49 Michael Fogden/DRK PHOTO. 50-51 (art), Tony Chen. 50 (art, center right), Robert Cremins. 50 (top right), Stephen Dalton/NHPA. 51 Michael Fogden. 52 (left) Dwight R. Kuhn/DRK PHOTO. 52 (bottom), G.I. Bernard/OXFORD SCIENTIFIC FILMS. 52-53, Jeff Foott. 53 (bottom), Frans Lanting/MINDEN PICTURES. 53 (art), Robert Cremins. 54 (top), George H. Harrison/GRANT HEILMAN. 54 (center), Stephen Dalton/NHPA. 54 (art), Robert Cremins. 55 Stephen Dalton/NHPA.

Back Matter: 56-57 (art), Robert Cremins. 56 ANIMALS ANIMALS/Michael Fogden. 57 (top), Michael & Patricia Fogden. 57 (bottom), Mary Clay/PLANET EARTH PICTURES. 60 Michael & Patricia Fogden.

Library of Congress CIP Data
Howell, Catherine Herbert.
    Reptiles & amphibians / by Catherine Herbert Howell.
        p.   cm — (National Geographic nature library)
    Includes index.
    Summary: Discusses what reptiles and amphibians are and examines the characteristics and behavior of lizards, snakes, turtles, crocodiles, alligators, frogs, toads, and salamanders.
    ISBN 0-7922-7042-8
    1. Reptiles—Juvenile literature. 2. Amphibians—Juvenile literature. [1. Reptiles. 2. Amphibians.]   I. Title. II. Title: Reptiles and amphibians. III. Series.
    QL644.2.H69 1993
    597.6—dc20   93-10735
                                                                            CIP
                                                                            AC